THIS BOOK IS FOR

....

BORN

....

LOTS OF LOVE
FOREVER & ALWAYS

....